CONTENTS

PREFACE

At March 2016, The British Ornithologists' Union Records Committee had 600 species of wild birds on its British list and each one is illustrated and described in this catalogue in addition there are eleven further additions and amendments.

The catalogue is designed for every level of ornithologist. The beginner will find its basic information all he needs to start out with, while the seasoned watcher will use it as a ready *aide-memoire* to jot down the essential information to be followed up in detail later.

A check list has not the room to go into full detail and much information has to be compressed. The geographic locations, for instance, can only give the most likely places to see the individual bird in the full knowledge that examples will be found outside the areas designated.

The list is arranged in alphabetical order of common names aided by a full index.

Every effort has been made to ensure the accuracy of the following pages but if any errors are found they are down to the editor and he would be happy to be contacted and put right.

Alan Avery

BIRDS OF THE BRITISH ISLES

An Illustrated Check List

Blackthorn Press

Blackthorn Press, Blackthorn House
Middleton Rd, Pickering YO18 8AL
United Kingdom

www.blackthornpress.com

ISBN 978 1 906259 45 7

© 2016

All rights reserved. No part of this publication may be reproduced, stored in a retrieval system or transmitted, in any form or by any means, electronic, mechanical, photocopying, recording, or otherwise, without the prior permission of the Blackthorn Press.

ILLUSTRATION CREDITS

The illustrations are by Raymond Harris Ching, Robert Gillmor and Hermann Heinzel by kind permission of the Automobile Association and the Reader's Digest Association Limited and by David Allen Sibley. Every effort has been made to identify other illustrations used. Enquiries about illustration rights should be addressed to the publishers.

REFERENCES

Websites

www.bou.org.uk/british-list/
The British Ornithologists' Union British List

www.hbw.com
Contains material for all the world's birds. Very
comprehensive but requires a subscription.

www.birdguides.com
A very good source for British birds. Many of the
entries are incomplete and it requires a subscription
for the full service.

www.rspb.org.uk/discoverandenjoynature/discoveran
dlearn/birdguide/name/
The RSPB's website. Excellent for most of the common
birds.

www.bbc.co.uk/programmes/b01s6xyk
The BBC's 'Tweet of the Day'. Excellent sound,
photographs and commentary.

Books

A good companion to this check list is *Collins Complete
Guide to British Birds.* It is not complete but contains a
further reading section. There are many books
available for every speciality.

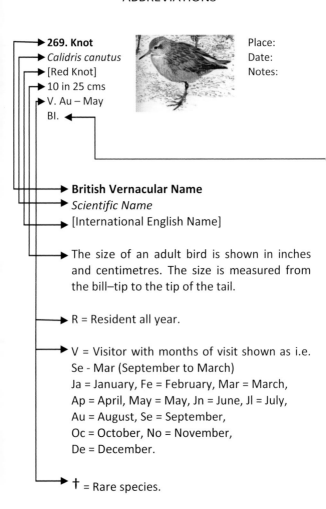

269. Knot
Calidris canutus
[Red Knot]
10 in 25 cms
V. Au – May
Bl.

Place:
Date:
Notes:

British Vernacular Name
Scientific Name
[International English Name]

The size of an adult bird is shown in inches and centimetres. The size is measured from the bill–tip to the tip of the tail.

R = Resident all year.

V = Visitor with months of visit shown as i.e.
Se - Mar (September to March)
Ja = January, Fe = February, Mar = March,
Ap = April, May = May, Jn = June, Jl = July,
Au = August, Se = September,
Oc = October, No = November,
De = December.

† = Rare species.

The main areas where a bird is to be found are shown
as: BI = British Isles, S = Scotland,
N = Northern England, W = Wales,
M = Midlands, SW = South West England,
SE = South East England, I = Ireland.

1. Alder Flycatcher
Empidonax alnorum
6¾ in 17 cms
V. Se – Oc
SE, SW.†

Place:
Date:
Notes:

2. Aleutian Tern
Onychoprion aleuticus
13½ in 34 cms
V. May
N. †

Place:
Date:
Notes:

3. Allen's Gallinule
Porphyrio alleni
9½ in 24 cms
V. Ja – Fe
SE, SW. †

Place:
Date:
Notes:

4. Alpine Accentor
Prunella collaris
7 in 18 cms
V. Ja – De
M, N, SE, SW, W. †

Place:
Date:
Notes:

5. Alpine Swift
Apus melba
9 in 23 cms
V. Mar – May
BI.

Place:
Date:
Notes:

6. American Bittern
Botaurus lentiginosus
30 in 75 cms
V. Se – May
Bl. †

Place:
Date:
Notes:

7. American Coot
Fulica americana
17 in 43 cms
V. No – Ap
I, N, S, SE. †

Place:
Date:
Notes:

8. American Golden Plover
Pluvialis dominica
11 in 28 cms
V. Jl – No
I, N, S, SE, SW.

Place:
Date:
Notes:

9. American Herring Gull
Larus smithsonianus
26 in 66 cms
V. De – Apr
I, N, S, SE, SW. †

Place:
Date:
Notes:

10. American Kestrel
Falco sparverius
8¼ in 21 cms
V. May – Jn
S, SW. †

Place:
Date:
Notes:

11. American Redstart
Setophaga ruticilla
5½ in 14 cms
V. Oc – No
I, M, S, SE, SW. †

Place:
Date:
Notes:

12. American Robin
Turdus migratorius
11 in 28 cms
V. Oc – Jn
Bl. †

Place:
Date:
Notes:

13. American Wigeon
Anas americana
24 in 59 cms
V. Se – May
I, N, S, SW.

Place:
Date:
Notes:

14. Amur Falcon
Falco amurensis
12 in 30 cms
V. Se
N. †

Place:
Date:
Notes:

15. Ancient Murrelet
Synthliboramphus antiquus
10¾ in 27 cms
V. May
SW. †

Place:
Date:
Notes:

16. Aquatic Warbler
Acrocephalus paludicola
5 in 13 cms
V. Au – Oc
I, SE, SW.

Place:
Date:
Notes:

17. Arctic Redpoll
Acanthis hornemanni
5½ in 14 cms
V. No – Mar
I, N, S.

Place:
Date:
Notes:

18. Arctic Skua
Stercorarius parasiticus
[Parasitic Jaeger]
18 in 45 cms
V. Jn – No
BI.

Place:
Date:
Notes

19. Arctic Tern
Sterna paradisaea
15 in 38 cms
V. Ap – Se
I, N, S, W.

Place:
Date:
Notes:

20. Arctic Warbler
Phylloscopus borealis
4¾ in 12 cms
V. Au – Oc
BI. †

Place:
Date:
Notes:

21. Ascension Frigatebird
Fregata aquila
39 in 96 cms
V. Jl
S. †

Place:
Date:
Notes:

22. Audouin's Gull
Larus audouinii
20 in 50 cms
V. May – Oc
M, N, SE, SW. †

Place:
Date:
Notes:

23. Avocet
Recurvirostra avosetta
[Pied Avocet]
17 in 42 cms
R.
M, N, SE, SW.

Place:
Date:
Notes:

24. Baikal Teal
Anas formosa
17 in 43 cms
V. Oc – Ap
I, M, N, SE. †

Place:
Date:
Notes:

25. Baillon's Crake
Porzana pusilla
7 in 18 cms
V. Ja – De
Bl. †

Place:
Date:
Notes:

26. Baird's Sandpiper
Calidris bairdii
7½ in 19 cms
V. Au – Oc
BI. †

Place:
Date:
Notes:

27. Balearic Shearwater
Puffinus mauretanicus
13 in 33 cms
V. Jl – Se
N, SE, SW, W.

Place:
Date:
Notes:

28. Baltimore Oriole
Icterus galbula
8½ in 22 cms
V. Se – Mar
I, S, SE, SW, W. †

Place:
Date:
Notes:

29. Barn Owl
Tyto alba
[Western Barn Owl]
13½ in 34 cms
R.
BI.

Place:
Date:
Notes:

30. Barnacle Goose
Branta leucopsis
27 in 68 cms
V. Oc – Mar
I, N, S.

Place:
Date:
Notes:

31. Barred Warbler
Sylvia nisoria
6¾ in 17 cms
V. Au – Oc
I, M, N, S, SE.

Place:
Date:
Notes:

32. Barrow's Goldeneye
Bucephala islandica
19 in 47 cms
V. May & No
I, S. †

Place:
Date:
Notes:

33. Bar-tailed Godwit
Limosa lapponica
15 in 38 cms
V. No – Fe
BI.

Place:
Date:
Notes:

34. Bay-breasted Warbler
Setophaga castanea
6 in 15 cms
V. Oc
SW. †

Place:
Date:
Notes:

35. Bean Goose
Anser fabalis
[Taiga / Tundra Bean Goose]
35 in 88 cms
V. Se - Mar
S, SE.

Place:
Date:
Notes:

36. Bearded Tit
Panurus biarmicus
[Bearded Reedling]
6½ in 16 cm
R.
M, N, SE, SW.

Place:
Date:
Notes:

37. Bee-eater
Merops apiaster
[European Bee-eater]
11 in 28 cms
V. Jn - Se
M, N, S, SE, SW.

Place:
Date:
Notes:

38. Belted Kingfisher
Megaceryle alcyon
14 in 35 cms
V. Oc – Ap
I, M, N, S, SW. †

Place:
Date:
Notes:

39. Bewick's Swan
Cygnus columbianus
[Tundra Swan]
56 in 140 cms
V. Oc – Mar
I, M, N, SE, SW, W. †

Place:
Date:
Notes:

40. Bimaculated Lark
Melanocorypha bimaculata
7 in 18 cms
V. May – Jn, Oc
S, SW. †

Place:
Date:
Notes:

41. Bittern
Botaurus stellaris
[Eurasian Bittern]
30 in 75 cm
R.
N, SE, SW, W.

Place:
Date:
Notes:

42. Black Duck
Anas rubripes
[American Black
Duck]
24 in 60 cms
V. Se – Jn
I, N, S, SE, SW, W. †

Place:
Date:
Notes:

43. Black Grouse
Tetrao tetrix
21 in 53 cms
R.
N, S, W.

Place:
Date:
Notes:

**44. Black
Guillemot**
Cepphus grylle
13½ in 34 cms
R.
S, I.

Place:
Date:
Notes:

45. Black Kite
Milvus migrans
24 in 60 cms
V. Apr – Au
BI.

Place:
Date:
Notes:

46. Black Lark
Melanocorypha
yeltoniensis
8 in 20 cms
V. Ap – Jn
N, SE, W. †

Place
Date:
Notes:

47. Black
Redstart
Phoenicurus
ochruros
5½ in 14 cms
V/R. Mar – Oc
M, N, SE, SW, W.

Place:
Date:
Notes:

48. Black Scoter
Melanitta
americana
18 in 45 cms
V. Oc – Jn
N, S, W. †

Place:
Date:
Notes:

49. Black Stork
Ciconia nigra
40 in 100 cms
V. Ap – No
Bl. †

Place:
Date:
Notes:

50. Black Tern
Chlidonias niger
10 in 25 cms
V. May – Se
Bl.

Place:
Date:
Notes:

51. Black-and-white Warbler
Mniotilta varia
5½ in 14 cms
V. Se – Mar
I, S, SE, SW, W. †

Place:
Date:
Notes:

52. Black-billed Cuckoo
Coccyzus erythropthalmus
12½ in 32 cms
V. Au – No
I, N, S, SW. †

Place:
Date:
Notes:

53. Blackbird
Turdus merula
[Common Blackbird]
10 in 25 cms
R.
Bl.

Place:
Date:
Notes:

54. Black-browed Albatross
Thalassarche melanophris
38 in 95 cm
V. Fe - De
Bl. †

Place:
Date:
Notes:

55. Blackburnian Warbler
Setophaga fusca
5 in 13 cms
V. Se - Oc
S, W. †

Place:
Date:
Notes:

56. Blackcap
Sylvia atricapilla
[Eurasian Blackcap]
5 in 13 cms
R.
Bl.

Place:
Date:
Notes:

57. Black-eared Wheatear
Oenanthe hispanica
6 in 15 cms
V. Mar – No
Bl. †

Place:
Date:
Notes:

58. Black-faced Bunting
Emberiza spodocephala
6 in 15 cms
V. Mar & Oc
N, S, SW. †

Place:
Date:
Notes:

59. Black-headed Bunting
Emberiza melanocephala
6 in 15 cms
V. Ap – No
Bl. †

Place:
Date:
Notes:

60. Black-headed Gull
Chroicocephalus ridibundus
15 in 38 cm
R.
Bl.

Place:
Date:
Notes:

61. Black-necked Grebe
Podiceps nigricollis
12 in 30 cms
R.
M, N, S, SE, SW, W.

Place:
Date:
Notes:

62. Blackpoll Warbler
Setophaga striata
6 in 15 cms
V. Se – No
I, N, S, SE, SW, W. †

Place:
Date:
Notes:

63. Black-tailed Godwit
Limosa limosa
15 in 38 cms
V. Jn - Fe
BI.

Place:
Date:
Notes:

64. Black-throated Diver
Gavia arctica
[Black-throated Loon]
27 in 68 cms
V. Jn - Fe
I, M, N, S, SE, SW.

Place:
Date:
Notes:

65. Black-throated Thrush
Turdus atrogularis
10¾ in 27 cms
V. Se – May
M, N, S, SE, SW. †

Place:
Date:
Notes:

66. Black-winged Pratincole
Glareola nordmanni
11 in 28 cms
V. May – No
Bl. †

Place:
Date:
Notes:

67. Black-winged Stilt
Himantopus himantopus
14 in 35 cms
V. Mar – De
Bl. †

Place:
Date:
Notes:

68. Blue Rock Thrush
Monticola solitarius
9 in 23 cms
V. Ap – Jn & Oc
S, SW, W. †

Place:
Date:
Notes:

69. Blue Tit
Cyanistes caeruleus
[Eurasian Blue Tit]
4½ in 11 cms
R.
Bl.

Place:
Date:
Notes:

70. Blue-cheeked Bee-eater
Merops persicus
12 in 31 cms
V. Jn – Se
M, N, S, SE, SW. †

Place:
Date:
Notes:

71. Bluethroat
Luscinia svecica
5½ in 14 cms
V. May – Oc
I, M, N, S, SE, W.

Place:
Date:
Notes:

72. Blue-winged Teal
Anas discors
16 in 40 cms
V. Ja – De
Bl. †

Place:
Date:
Notes:

73. Blyth's Pipit
Anthus godlewskii
6¾ in 17 cms
V. Se – De
M, N, S, SE, SW, W.†

Place:
Date:
Notes:

74. Blyth's Reed Warbler
Acrocephalus dumetorum
5½ in 14 cms
V. Se – Oc
M, N, S, SE, SW, W. †

Place:
Date:
Notes:

75. Bobolink
Dolichonyx oryzivorus
7 in 18 cms
V. Se – No
I, N, S, SW, W. †

Place:
Date:
Notes:

76. Bonaparte's Gull
Chroicocephalus philadelphia
15 in 38 cms
V. Ja – De
BI. †

Place:
Date:
Notes:

77. Booted Warbler
Iduna caligata
4¾ in 12 cms
V. Jn – No
BI. †

Place:
Date:
Notes:

78. Brambling
Fringilla montifringilla
5¾ in 14.5 cms
V. Se – Ap
BI.

Place:
Date:
Notes:

79. Brent Goose
Branta bernicla
[Brant Goose]
24 in 60 cms
V. Oc – Mar
I, M, N, SE.

Place:
Date:
Notes:

80. Bridled Tern
Onychoprion anaethetus
12½ in 32 cms
V. Ap – No
M, N, S, SE, SW, W. †

Place:
Date:
Notes:

81. Broad-billed Sandpiper
Calidris falcinellus
7 in 18 cms
V. May – Se
BI. †

Place:
Date:
Notes:

82. Brown Flycatcher
Muscicapa dauurica
[Asian Brown Flycatcher]
5 in 13 cms
V. Jn - Oc
N, S. †

Place:
Date:
Notes:

83. Brown Shrike
Lanius cristatus
8 in 20 cms
V. Se – No
I, N, S, SE, SW. †

Place:
Date:
Notes:

84. Brown Skua
Stercorarius antarcticus
26 in 64 cms
V. Fe & Oc
SW, W. †

Place:
Date:
Notes:

85. Brown Thrasher
Toxostoma rufum
12 in 30 cms
V. No
SW. †

Place:
Date:
Notes:

86. Brown-headed Cowbird
Molothrus ater
8½ in 22 cms
V. Apr – Jl
N, S, W. †

Place:
Date:
Notes:

87. Brünnich's Guillemot
Uria lomvia
[Thick-billed Murre]
19½ in 48 cms
V. Oc – Jl
I, N, S, SW. †

Place:
Date:
Notes:

88. Buff-bellied Pipit
Anthus rubescens
6¾ in 17 cms
V. Se – De
I, M, N, S, SE, SW. †

Place:
Date:
Notes:

89. Buff-breasted Sandpiper
Calidris subruficollis
8 in 20 cms
V. Se – No
BI.

Place:
Date:
Notes:

90. Bufflehead
Bucephala albeola
16 in 40 cms
V. Oc – Jn
I, M, N, S, SE, SW. †

Place:
Date:
Notes:

91. Bullfinch
Pyrrhula pyrrhula
[Eurasian
Bullfinch]
5¾ in 14.5 cms
R.
Bl.

Place:
Date:
Notes:

92. Buzzard
Buteo buteo
[Common
Buzzard]
22 in 55 cms
R.
Bl.

Place:
Date:
Notes:

93. Cabot's Tern
Sterna acuflavida
17 in 42 cms
V. No
M. †

Place:
Date:
Notes:

94. Calandra Lark
*Melanocorypha
calandra*
8 in 20 cms
V. Ap - May
M, N, S, SE, SW. †

Place:
Date:
Notes:

95. Canvasback
Aythya valisineria
23 in 56 cms
V. De – Jl
N, S, SE, SW. †

Place:
Date:
Notes:

**96. Cape May
Warbler**
Setophaga tigrina
5½ in 14 cms
V. Jn & Oc
S. †

Place:
Date:
Notes:

**97. Cape Verde
Storm Petrel**
*Oceanodroma
jabejabe*
8¼ in 21 cms
V. Jl - Oc
I, SW. †

Place:
Date:
Notes:

98. Capercaillie
Tetrao urogallus
[Western
Capercaillie]
33 in 83 cms
R.
S.

Place:
Date:
Notes:

99. Capped Petrel
*Pterodroma
hasitata*
[Black-capped
Petrel]
16 in 40 cm
V. De & Mar
N, SE. †

Place:
Date:
Notes:

**100. Carrion
Crow**
Corvus corone
18½ in 46 cms
R.
M, N, S, SE, SW, W.

Place:
Date:
Notes:

101. Caspian Gull
Larus cachinnans
27 in 68 cms
V. Ja – De
M, N SE.

Place:
Date:
Notes:

102. Caspian Plover
Charadrius asiaticus
8 in 20 cms
V. May - Jl
S, SE, SW. †

Place:
Date:
Notes:

103. Caspian Tern
Hydroprogne caspia
21 in 53 cms
V. Ap – Oc
BI.

Place:
Date:
Notes:

104. Cattle Egret
Bubulcus ibis
[Western Cattle Egret]
23 in 56 cms
V. Ja - De
SE, SW, W.

Place:
Date:
Notes:

105. Cedar Waxwing
Bombycilla cedrorum
7 in 18 cms
V. Fe – No
I, M, S. †

Place:
Date:
Notes:

106. Cetti's Warbler
Cettia cetti
5½ in 14 cms
R.
SE, SW, W.

Place:
Date:
Notes:

107. Chaffinch
Fringilla coelebs
[Common Chaffinch]
6 in 15 cms
R.
Bl.

Place:
Date:
Notes:

108. Chestnut-eared Bunting
Emberiza fucata
6½ in 16 cms
V. Oc
S. †

Place:
Date:
Notes:

109. Chestnut-sided Warbler
Setophaga pensylvanica
5½ in 14 cms
V. Oc
S, SW. †

Place:
Date:
Notes:

110. Chiffchaff
Phylloscopus collybita
[Common Chiffchaff]
4¼ in 10 cms
R.
Bl.

Place:
Date:
Notes:

111. Chimney Swift
Chaetura pelagica
6 in 15 cms
V. Oc – No
I, M, N, S, SW, W. †

Place:
Date:
Notes:

112. Chough
Pyrrhocorax pyrrhocorax
[Red-billed Chough]
15 in 38 cms
R.
I, S, W.

Place:
Date:
Notes:

113. Cirl Bunting
Emberiza cirlus
6½ in 16 cms
R.
BI.

Place:
Date:
Notes:

114. Citril Finch
Carduelis citrinella
4¾ in 12 cms
V. May - Jn
S, SE. †

Place:
Date:
Notes:

115. Citrine Wagtail
Motacilla citreola
6¾ in 17 cms
V. Au – Oc
N, S. †

Place:
Date:
Notes:

116. Cliff Swallow
Petrochelidon pyrrhonota
[American Cliff Swallow]
5½ in 14 cms
V. Se - De
I, N, SE, SW. †

Place:
Date:
Notes:

117. Coal Tit
Periparus ater
4¼ in 10 cms
R.
Bl.

Place:
Date:
Notes:

118. Collared Dove
Streptopelia decaocto
[Eurasian Collared Dove]
12½ in 32 cm
R.
Bl.

Place:
Date:
Notes:

119. Collared Flycatcher
Ficedula albicollis
5 in 13 cms
V. Ap – Jn
I, N, S, SE, SW, W. †

Place:
Date:
Notes:

120. Collared Pratincole
Glareola pratincola
11 in 28 cms
V. Ap - No
Bl. †

Place:
Date:
Notes:

**121. Common
Gull**
Larus canus
[Mew Gull]
17 in 42 cms
R.
BI.

Place:
Date:
Notes:

**122. Common
Nighthawk**
Chordeiles minor
10 in 25 cms
V. Se – Oc
BI. †

Place:
Date:
Notes:

**123. Common
Redpoll**
Acanthis flammea
5 in 13 cms
R.
BI.

Place:
Date:
Notes:

**124. Common
Rosefinch**
*Erythrina
erythrina*
6 in 15 cms
V. Jn – No
I, S, SW.

Place:
Date:
Notes:

**125. Common
Sandpiper**
Actitis hypoleucos
8 in 20 cms
V. Ja – De
BI.

Place:
Date:
Notes:

**126. Common
Scoter**
Melanitta nigra
19 in 47 cms
V. Ja – De
BI.

Place:
Date:
Notes:

**127. Common
Tern**
Sterna hirundo
14 in 36 cms
V. Ap – Au
BI.

Place:
Date:
Notes:

**128. Common
Yellowthroat**
Geothlypis trichas
6 in 15 cms
V. Se – Jn
I, S, SE, SW, W. †

Place:
Date:
Notes:

129. Coot
Fulica atra
[Eurasian Coot]
15 in 38 cms
R.
BI.

Place:
Date:
Notes:

130. Cormorant
*Phalacrocorax
carbo*
[Great
Cormorant]
36 in 90 cms
R.
BI.

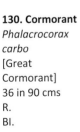

Place:
Date:
Notes:

131. Corn Bunting
Emberiza calandra
7 in 18 cms
R.
M, N, S, SE, SW, W.

Place:
Date:
Notes:

132. Corncrake
Crex crex
[Corn Crake]
10½ in 26 cms
V. Apr – Se
I, S.

Place:
Date:
Notes:

133. Cory's Shearwater
Calonectris borealis
23 in 56 cms
V. Jl – Oc
I, SW.

Place:
Date:
Notes:

134. Crag Martin
Ptyonoprogne rupestris
[Eurasian Crag Martin]
5½ in 14 cms
V. Ap – Oc
M, N, S, SE, SW, W. †

Place:
Date:
Notes:

135. Crane
Grus grus
[Common Crane]
52 in 130 cms
V. Apr – Oc
SE.

Place:
Date:
Notes:

136. Cream-coloured Courser
Cursorius cursor
8½ in 22 cms
V. Se – De
BI. †

Place:
Date:
Notes:

137. Crested Lark
Galerida cristata
6¾ in 17 cms
V. Mar – Dec
N, S, SE, SW, W. †

Place:
Date:
Notes:

138. Crested Tit
Lophophanes cristatus
[European Crested Tit]
4½ in 11 cms
R.
S.

Place:
Date:
Notes:

139. Cretzschmar's Bunting
Emberiza caesia
6½ in 16 cms
V. Ap – Se
S. †

Place:
Date:
Notes:

140. Crossbill
Loxia curvirostra
[Red Crossbill]
6¾ in 17 cms
R.
BI.

Place:
Date:
Notes:

141. Cuckoo
Cuculus canorus
[Common Cuckoo]
13 in 33 cms
V. Mar – Au
BI.

Place:
Date:
Notes:

142. Curlew
Numenius arquata
[Eurasian Curlew]
22 in 55 cms
R.
BI.

Place:
Date:
Notes:

143. Curlew Sandpiper
Calidris ferruginea
7½ in 19 cms
V. Au – Se
BI.

Place:
Date:
Notes:

144. Dark-eyed Junco
Junco hyemalis
6¾ in 17 cms
V. No – Ap
BI. †

Place:
Date:
Notes:

145. Dartford Warbler
Sylvia undata
5 in 13 cms
R.
SE, SW.

Place:
Date:
Notes:

146. Daurian Shrike
Lanius isabellinus isabellinus
7 in 18 cm
V. Sep
I, N, S, SE, SW. †

Place:
Date:
Notes:

147. Desert Warbler
Sylvia nana / deserti
[Asian Desert Warbler]
5 in 12.5 cm
V. Mar – De
N, SE, SW. †

Place:
Date:
Notes:

148. Desert Wheatear
Oenanthe deserti
6 in 15 cms
V. Oc – Ap
Bl. †

Place:
Date:
Notes:

149. Dipper
Cinclus cinclus
[White-throated Dipper]
7 in 18 cms
R.
I, M, N, S, SW, W.

Place:
Date:
Notes:

150. Dotterel
Charadrius morinellus
[Eurasian Dotterel]
8½ in 22 cms
V. Ap – Se
S, SE.

Place:
Date:
Notes:

151. Double-crested Cormorant
Phalacrocorax auritus
35 in 88 cms
V. No & Ja
I, N. †

Place:
Date:
Notes:

152. Dunlin
Calidris alpina
7 in 18 cms
R.
BI.

Place:
Date:
Notes:

153. Dunnock
Prunella modularis
5¾ in 14.5 cms
R.
BI.

Place:
Date:
Notes:

154. Dusky Thrush
Turdus eunomus
10 in 25 cms
V. Se – May
M, N, S, SE, SW, W. †

Place:
Date:
Notes:

155. Dusky Warbler
Phylloscopus fuscatus
4½ in 11 cms
V. Oc – Ja
SE, SW.

Place:
Date:
Notes:

156. Eastern Bonelli's Warbler
Phylloscopus orientalis
4½ in 11.5 cms
V. Ap – Oc
N, S, SW. †

Place:
Date:
Notes:

157. Eastern Crowned Warbler
Phylloscopus coronatus
4¾ in 12 cms
V. Oc
N, SE. †

Place:
Date:
Notes:

158. Eastern Olivaceous Warbler
Iduna pallida
5½ in 14 cms
V. May - Oc
I, N, S, SE, SW. †

Place:
Date:
Notes:

159. Eastern Phoebe
Sayornis phoebe
4½ in 11 cms
V. Apr
SW. †

Place:
Date:
Notes:

**160. Eastern
Towhee**
*Pipilo
erythrophthalmus*
9 in 23 cms
V. Jn
SW. †

Place:
Date:
Notes:

**161. Egyptian
Goose**
*Alopochen
aegyptiaca*
29 in 73 cms
R.
SE.

Place:
Date:
Notes:

**162. Egyptian
NIghtjar**
*Caprimulgus
aegyptius*
10 in 25 cms
V. Ju
M, SW. †

Place:
Date:
Notes:

**163. Egyptian
Vulture**
*Neophron
percnopterus*
26 in 65 cms
V. Se - Oc
SE, SW. †

Place:
Date:
Notes:

164. Eider
*Somateria
mollissima*
[Common Eider]
24 in 60 cms
R.
BI.

Place:
Date:
Notes:

165. Eleonora's Falcon
Falco eleonorae
17 in 42 cms
V. Ju - Oc
N, S, SE, SW. †

Place:
Date:
Notes:

166. Eskimo Curlew
Numenius borealis
12 in 30 cms
V. Se – Oc
I, S, SW. †

Place:
Date:
Notes: Extinct?

167. Evening Grosbeak
Hesperiphona vespertina
8½ in 22 cms
V. Mar
S. †

Place:
Date:
Notes:

168. Eyebrowed Thrush
Turdus obscurus
9 in 23 cms
V. Ap – De
M, N, S, SW, W. †

Place:
Date:
Notes:

169. Fan-tailed Warbler
Cisticola juncidis
[Zitting Cisticola]
6½ in 16 cms
V. Mar – Se
I, SE, SW. †

Place:
Date:
Notes:

170. Fea's Petrel
Pterodroma feae
14 in 36 cms
V. Jl – Se
SW. †

Place:
Date:
Notes:

171. Ferruginous Duck
Aythya nyroca
16 in 40 cms
V. Se – Fe
SE.

Place:
Date:
Notes:

172. Fieldfare
Turdus pilaris
10 in 25 cms
V. Oc – May
BI.

Place:
Date:
Notes:

173. Firecrest
Regulus ignicapilla
[Common Firecrest]
3½ in 9 cms
R.
SE, SW, W.

Place:
Date:
Notes:

174. Forster's Tern
Sterna forsteri
14 in 36 cms
V. Ja – De
I, N, S, SE, SW, W. †

Place:
Date:
Notes:

175. Franklin's Gull
Larus pipixcan
14 in 36 cms
V. Ja – De
BI. †

Place:
Date:
Notes:

176. Frigate Petrel
Pelagodroma marina
[White-faced Storm Petrel]
8¼ in 21 cms
V. Ja
S. †

Place:
Date:
Notes:

177. Fulmar
Fulmarus glacialis
[Northern Fulmar]
18½ in 46 cms
R.
BI.

Place:
Date:
Notes:

178. Gadwall
Anas strepera
20 in 50 cms
R.
I, S, M, SE, SW, W.

Place:
Date:
Notes:

179. Gannet
Morus bassanus
[Northern Gannet]
36 in 90 cms
R.
BI.

Place:
Date:
Notes:

180. Garden Warbler
Sylvia borin
5½ in 14 cms
V. Apr – Se
BI.

Place:
Date:
Notes:

181. Garganey
Anas querquedula
15 in 38 cms
V. Mar – Jl
M, N, S, SE, SW, W.

Place:
Date:
Notes:

182. Glaucous Gull
Larus hyperboreus
27 in 68 cms
V. No – Mar
BI.

Place:
Date:
Notes:

183. Glaucous-winged Gull
Larus glaucescens
27 in 68 cms
V. De - Ja
I, M, N, SE, W. †

Place:
Date:
Notes:

184. Glossy Ibis
Plegadis falcinellus
22 in 55 cms
V. No – Ja
I, SE, SW.

Place:
Date:
Notes:

185. Goldcrest
Regulus regulus
3½ in 9 cms
R.
Bl.

Place:
Date:
Notes:

186. Golden Eagle
Aquila chrysaetos
35 in 88 cms
R.
N, S.

Place:
Date:
Notes:

187. Golden Oriole
Oriolus oriolus
[Eurasian Golden Oriole]
9½ in 24 cms
V. May – Au
SE.

Place:
Date:
Notes:

188. Golden Pheasant
Chrysolophus pictus
23 in 56 cms
R.
S, SE, SW, W.

Place:
Date:
Notes:

189. Golden Plover
Pluvialis apricaria
[European Golden Plover]
11 in 28 cms
R.
Bl.

Place:
Date:
Notes:

190. Goldeneye
Bucephala
clangula
[Common
Goldeneye]
18 in 45 cms
R/V. De – Fe
BI.

Place:
Date:
Notes:

**191. Golden-
winged Warbler**
Vermivora
chrysoptera
4¾ in 11.5 cms
V. Ja
SE. †

Place:
Date:
Notes:

192. Goldfinch
Carduelis
carduelis
[European
Goldfinch]
4¾ in 11.5 cms
R.
BI.

Place:
Date:
Notes:

193. Goosander
Mergus
merganser
[Common
Merganser]
26 in 64 cms
R.
M, N, S, SE, SW, W.

Place:
Date:
Notes:

194. Goshawk
Accipiter gentilis
[Northern
Goshawk]
21 in 53 cms
R.
M, N, S, SE, SW, W.

Place:
Date:
Notes:

**195. Grasshopper
Warbler**
Locustella naevia
[Common
Grasshopper
Warbler]
5 in 13 cms
V. Ap – Se
BI.

Place:
Date:
Notes:

196. Great Auk
Pinguinus impennis
34 in 85 cms
May
I, S.

Place:
Date:
Notes: Extinct

**197. Great Black-
backed Gull**
Larus marinus
27 in 68 cms
R.
BI.

Place:
Date:
Notes:

**198. Great Black-
headed Gull**
Larus ichthyaetus
[Pallas's Gull]
29 in 72 cms
V. May
SW. †

Place:
Date:
Notes:

**199. Great Blue
Heron**
Ardea herodias
56 in 140 cms
V. De
SW. †

Place:
Date:
Notes:

**200. Great
Bustard**
Otis tarda
40 in 100 cms
V. De – Mar
Bl. †

Place:
Date:
Notes:

**201. Great
Crested Grebe**
Podiceps cristatus
19 in 47 cms
R.
Bl.

Place:
Date:
Notes:

**202. Great Grey
Shrike**
Lanius excubitor
9½ in 24 cms
V. Se – May
M, N, S, SE.

Place:
Date:
Notes:

203. Great Knot
*Calidris
tenuirostris*
10¾ in 27 cms
V. Jl – Oc
I, N, S, SE. †

Place:
Date:
Notes:

**204. Great
Northern Diver**
Gavia immer
[Great Northern
Loon]
33 in 83 cms
V. Au – May
Bl.

Place:
Date:
Notes:

**205. Great Reed
Warbler**
*Acrocephalus
arundinaceus*
7½ in 19 cms
V. Ap – No
Bl. †

Place:
Date:
Notes:

**206. Great
Shearwater**
Puffinus gravis
18 in 45 cms
V. Jl – Se
I, S, SW.

Place:
Date:
Notes:

207. Great Skua
Stercorarius skua
23 in 56 cms
V. Ap – Jl
Bl.

Place:
Date:
Notes

208. Great Snipe
Gallinago media
11 in 28 cms
V. Au – De
Bl. †

Place:
Date:
Notes:

**209. Great
Spotted Cuckoo**
*Clamator
glandarius*
15½ in 39 cms
V. Fe – Oc
Bl. †

Place:
Date:
Notes:

**210. Great
Spotted
Woodpecker**
*Dendrocopos
major*
9 in 23 cms
R.
M, N, S, SE, SW, W.

Place:
Date:
Notes:

211. Great Tit
Parus major
5½ in 14 cms
R.
Bl.

Place:
Date:
Notes:

**212. Great White
Egret**
Ardea alba
[Great Egret]
42 in 104 cms
V. De – May
Bl.

Place:
Date:
Notes:

**213. Greater
Canada Goose**
Branta canadensis
[Canada Goose]
38 in 95 cms
R.
Bl.

Place:
Date:
Notes:

**214. Greater
Sand Plover**
*Charadrius
leschenaultii*
10 in 25 cms
V. Ap – De
M, N, S, SE, SW, W. †

Place:
Date:
Notes:

**215. Greater
Yellowlegs**
*Tringa
melanoleuca*
16 in 40 cms
V. Ja – De
Bl. †

Place:
Date:
Notes:

216. Green Heron
*Butorides
virescens*
17½ in 44 cms
V. Au – No
Bl. †

Place:
Date:
Notes:

**217. Green
Sandpiper**
Tringa ochropus
9 in 23 cms
V. Jl – Mar
I, M, N, SE, SW, W.

Place:
Date:
Notes:

**218. Green
Warbler**
*Phylloscopus
nitidus*
4¼ in 10 cms
V. Se
SW. †

Place:
Date:
Notes:

219. Green Woodpecker
Picus viridis
[European Green Woodpecker]
12½ in 32 cms
R.
M, N, S, SE, SE, W.

Place:
Date:
Notes:

220. Greenfinch
Chloris chloris
[European Greenfinch]
5¾ in 14.5 cms
R.
BI.

Place:
Date:
Notes:

221. Greenish Warbler
Phylloscopus trochiloides
[Two-barred Warbler]
4¼ in 10 cms
V. Jn – Se
M, N, S, SE.

Place:
Date:
Notes:

222. Greenshank
Tringa nebularia
[Common Greenshank]
12 in 30 cms
V. Ja - De
BI.

Place:
Date:
Notes:

223. Green-winged Teal
Anas carolinensis
14 in 36 cms
V. De – Mar
BI.

Place:
Date:
Notes:

224. Grey Catbird
Dumetella carolinensis
9½ in 24 cms
V. Oc – No
I, W. †

Place:
Date:
Notes:

225. Grey Heron
Ardea cinerea
39 in 98 cms
R.
BI.

Place:
Date:
Notes:

226. Grey Partridge
Perdix perdix
12 in 30 cms
R.
BI.

Place:
Date:
Notes:

227. Grey Phalarope
Phalaropus fulicarius
[Red Phalarope]
8 in 20 cms
V. Oc – Ja
I, M, N, SE, SW, W.

Place:
Date:
Notes:

228. Grey Plover
Pluvialis
squatarola
11 in 28 cms
V. No – May
BI.

Place:
Date:
Notes:

229. Grey Wagtail
Motacilla cinerea
8 in 20 cms
R.
BI.

Place:
Date:
Notes:

230. Grey-cheeked Thrush
Catharus minimus
6¾ in 17 cms
V. Se – No
I, N, S, SE, SW, W. †

Place:
Date:
Notes:

231. Greylag Goose
Anser anser
35 in 88 cms
R.
BI.

Place:
Date:
Notes:

232. Grey-tailed Tattler
Tringa brevipes
10¾ in 27 cms
V. Oc – No
S, W. †

Place:
Date:
Notes:

233. Guillemot
Uria aalge
[Common Murre]
16½ in 41 cms
V. Mar - Jl
I, N, S, SW, W.

Place:
Date:
Notes:

234. Gull-billed Tern
Gelochelidon nilotica
15 in 38 cms
V. Ap – Oc
Bl. †

Place:
Date:
Notes:

235. Gyr Falcon
Falco rusticolus
[Gyrfalcon]
21 in 53 cms
V. Ja – De
Bl. †

Place:
Date:
Notes:

236. Harlequin Duck
Histrionicus histrionicus
17 in 42 cms
V. Oc – Jn
N, S. †

Place:
Date:
Notes:

237. Hawfinch
Coccothraustes coccothraustes
7 in 18 cms
R.
M, N, S, SE, SW, W.

Place:
Date:
Notes:

238. Hawk Owl
Surnia ulula
[Northern Hawk
Owl]
17 in 42 cms
V. Se – Mar
S, SW. †

Place:
Date:
Notes:

239. Hen Harrier
Circus cyaneus
[Northern Harrier]
20 in 50 cms
R.
BI.

Place:
Date:
Notes:

**240. Hermit
Thrush**
Catharus guttatus
7 in 18 cms
V. Ap - Oc
I, S, SW. †

Place:
Date:
Notes:

241. Herring Gull
Larus argentatus
[European
Herring Gull]
23 in 58 cms
R.
BI.

Place:
Date:
Notes:

242. Hobby
Falco subbuteo
[Eurasian Hobby]
13 in 33 cms
V. Ap – Se
M, N, S, SE, SW, W.

Place:
Date:
Notes:

243. Honey-buzzard
Pernis apivorus
[European Honey Buzzard]
21½ in 54 cms
V. May – Au
M, S, SE, SW.

Place:
Date:
Notes:

244. Hooded Crow
Corvus cornix
18½ in 46 cms
R.
I, S.

Place:
Date:
Notes:

245. Hooded Merganser
Lophodytes cucullatus
19 in 47 cms
V. Oc – Ap
N, S, SE. †

Place:
Date:
Notes:

246. Hooded Warbler
Setophaga citrina
5 in 13 cms
V. Se
S, SW. †

Place:
Date:
Notes:

247. Hoopoe
Upupa epops
[Eurasian Hoopoe]
11½ in 29 cms
V. Ap – May
SE, SW.

Place:
Date:
Notes:

248. House Martin
Delichon urbicum
[Common House
Martin]
5 in 13 cms
V. Ap – Oc
BI.

Place:
Date:
Notes:

**249. House
Sparrow**
Passer domesticus
5¾ in 14.5 cms
R.
BI.

Place:
Date:
Notes:

**250. Hudsonian
Godwit**
Limosa haemastica
17 in 42 cms
V. Se
N, S, SW, †

Place:
Date:
Notes:

**251. Hudsonian
Whimbrel**
*Numenius
hudsonicus*
16 in 40 cms
V. May – Oc
I, N, S, SW, W. †

Place:
Date:
Notes

**252. Hume's
Warbler**
Phylloscopus humei
[Hume's Leaf
Warbler]
4½ in 11 cms
V. Oc – Fe
BI. †

Place:
Date:
Notes:

**253. Iberian
Chiffchaff**
*Phylloscopus
ibericus*
4¾ in 12 cms
V. Ap – Ju
BI. †

Place:
Date:
Notes:

254. Iceland Gull
Larus glaucoides
22 in 55 cms
V. De – Ap
BI.

Place:
Date:
Notes:

**255. Icterine
Warbler**
Hippolais icterina
5 in 13 cms
V. Au – No
M, N, S, SE.

Place:
Date:
Notes:

**256. Indigo
Bunting**
Passerina cyanea
5 in 13 cms
V. May & Oct
I, W. †

Place:
Date:
Notes:

**257. Isabelline
Shrike**
Lanius isabellinus
[Red-tailed Shrike]
8½ in 22 cms
V. Se – No
BI. †

Place:
Date:
Notes:

258. Isabelline
Wheatear
Oenanthe
isabellina
7 in 16.5 cms
V. Se – No
I, N, S, SE, SW, W. †

Place:
Date:
Notes:

259. Ivory Gull
Pagophila
eburnea
17½ in 44 cms
V. No – Mar
Bl. †

Place:
Date:
Notes:

260. Jack Snipe
Lymnocryptes
minimus
7½ in 19 cms
V. Se – Ap
Bl.

Place:
Date:
Notes:

261. Jackdaw
Corvus monedula
[Western Jackdaw]
13 in 33 cms
R.
Bl.

Place:
Date:
Notes:

262. Jay
Garrulus
glandarius
[Eurasian Jay]
13½ in 34 cms
R.
Bl.

Place:
Date:
Notes:

**263. Kentish
Plover**
*Charadrius
alexandrinus*
6½ in 16 cms
V. Ap – Se
SE, SW.

Place:
Date:
Notes:

264. Kestrel
Falco tinnunculus
[Common Kestrel]
14 in 36 cms
R.
BI.

Place:
Date:
Notes:

265. Killdeer
*Charadrius
vociferus*
10¾ in 27 cms
V. Se – May
BI. †

Place:
Date:
Notes:

266. King Eider
*Somateria
spectabilis*
22 in 55 cms
V. Ja – De
BI. †

Place:
Date:
Notes:

267. Kingfisher
Alcedo atthis
[Common
Kingfisher]
6½ in 16 cms
R.
BI.

Place:
Date:
Notes:

268. Kittiwake
Rissa tridactyla
[Black-legged
Kittiwake]
16 in 40 cms
R.
BI.

Place:
Date:
Notes:

269. Knot
Calidris canutus
[Red Knot]
10 in 25 cms
V. Au – May
BI.

Place:
Date:
Notes:

**270. Lady Amherst's
Pheasant**
*Chrysolophus
amherstiae*
23 in 56 cms
R.
SE.

Place:
Date:
Notes:

**271. Lanceolated
Warbler**
*Locustella
lanceolata*
4¾ in 12 cms
V. Se – No
M, N, S, SE, SW, W.†

Place:
Date:
Notes:

**272. Lapland
Bunting**
Calcarius lapponicus
[Lapland Longspur]
6 in 15 cms
V. Se – May
M, N, S, SE.

Place:
Date:
Notes:

273. Lapwing
Vanellus vanellus
[Northern Lapwing]
12 in 30 cms
R.
Bl.

Place:
Date:
Notes:

**274. Lark
Sparrow**
*Chondestes
grammacus*
6½ in 16 cms
V. May - Jn
SE. †

Place:
Date:
Notes:

275. Laughing Gull
Larus atricilla
16 in 40 cms
V. Ja – De
Bl. †

Place:
Date:
Notes:

**276. Leach's
Petrel**
*Oceanodroma
leucorhoa*
[Leach's Storm
Petrel]
8 in 20 cms
V. Jn – Au
I, S.

Place:
Date:
Notes:

**277 Least
Sandpiper**
Calidris minutilla
6 in 15 cms
V. May – Oc
Bl. †

Place:
Date:
Notes:

**278. Lesser Black-
backed Gull**
Larus fuscus
21 in 53 cms
R.
BI.

Place:
Date:
Notes:

**279. Lesser
Crested Tern**
*Sterna
bengalensis*
17 in 43 cms
V. Ap – Au
BI. †

Place:
Date:
Notes:

**280. Lesser Grey
Shrike**
Lanius minor
8 in 20 cms
V. May – Oc
BI. †

Place:
Date:
Notes:

**281. Lesser
Kestrel**
Falco naumanni
13 in 33 cms
V. Fe – No
I, N, S, SE, SW. †

Place:
Date:
Notes:

**282. Lesser
Redpoll**
Acanthis cabaret
[Common Redpoll]
5 in 13 cms
R.
BI.

Place:
Date:
Notes:

**283. Lesser Sand
Plover**
*Charadrius
mongolus*
8¼ in 21 cms
V. May – Au
I, M, S, SE. †

Place:
Date:
Notes:

284. Lesser Scaup
Aythya affinis
19½ in 48 cms
V. Jan – Dec
Bl. †

Place:
Date:
Notes:

**285. Lesser Short-
toed Lark**
Alaudala rufescens
5½ in 14 cms
V. May
SW. †

Place:
Date:
Notes:

**286. Lesser
Spotted
Woodpecker**
*Dendrocopos
minor*
5¾ in 14.5 cms
R.
M, N, SE, SW, W.

Place:
Date:
Notes:

**287. Lesser
White-fronted
Goose**
Anser erythropus
26 in 66 cms
V. De - Mar
Bl. †

Place:
Date:
Notes:

288. Lesser Whitethroat
Sylvia curruca
5¼ in 13.5 cms
V. Ap – Oc
M, N, S, SE, SW, W.

Place:
Date:
Notes:

289. Lesser Yellowlegs
Tringa flavipes
10¾ in 27 cms
V. Ap – No
BI. †

Place:
Date:
Notes:

290. Linnet
Linaria cannabina
[Common Linnet]
5¼ in 13.5 cms
R.
BI.

Place:
Date:
Notes:

291. Little Auk
Alle alle
8 in 20 cms
V. Oc – Fe
M, N, S, SE.

Place:
Date:
Notes:

292. Little Bittern
Ixobrychus minutus
14 in 36 cms
V. Mar – Oc
BI. †

Place:
Date:
Notes:

**293. Little
Bunting**
Emberiza pusilla
5¼ in 13.5 cms
V. Se – Mar
M, N, S, SE, SW.

Place:
Date:
Notes:

**294. Little
Bustard**
Tetrax tetrax
17 in 42 cms
V. Se – Fe
Bl. †

Place:
Date:
Notes:

295. Little Crake
Porzana parva
7½ in 19 cms
V. Mar – No
Bl. †

Place:
Date:
Notes:

296. Little Egret
Egretta garzetta
22 in 55 cms
V. Ja – De
Bl.

Place:
Date:
Notes:

297. Little Grebe
*Tachybaptus
ruficollis*
9 in 23 cms
R.
Bl.

Place:
Date:
Notes:

298. Little Gull
Hydrocoloeus
minutus
11 in 28 cms
V. Jl – Ap
BI.

Place:
Date:
Notes:

299. Little Owl
Athene noctua
8½ in 22 cms
R.
M, N, S, SE, SW, W.

Place:
Date:
Notes:

**300. Little Ringed
Plover**
Charadrius dubius
6 in 15 cms
V. Mar – Jul
M, N, SE, SW, W.

Place:
Date:
Notes:

301. Little Stint
Calidris minuta
5¼ in 13.5 cms
V. Ap – Se
BI.

Place:
Date:
Notes:

302. Little Swift
Apus affinis
4¾ in 12 cms
V. Ap – No
BI. †

Place:
Date:
Notes:

303. Little Tern
Sternula albifrons
[Least Tern]
9 in 23 cms
V. Ap – Se
BI.

Place:
Date:
Notes:

**304. Little
Whimbrel**
Numenius minutus
[Little Curlew]
12½ in 32 cms
V. Au
SE, W. †

Place:
Date:
Notes:

**305. Long-billed
Dowitcher**
*Limnodromus
scolopaceus*
11½ in 29 cms
V. Jl – No
BI. †

Place:
Date:
Notes:

**306. Long-billed
Murrelet**
*Brachyramphus
perdix*
10½ in 26 cms
V. No
SW. †

Place:
Date:
Notes:

**307. Long-eared
Owl**
Asio otus
14 in 36 cms
R.
BI.

Place:
Date:
Notes:

**308. Long-tailed
Duck**
Clangula hyemalis
23 in 58 cms
V. De – Fe
I, M, N, S, SE.

Place:
Date:
Notes:

**309. Long-tailed
Shrike**
Lanius schach
10 in 25 cms
V. No
S. †

Place:
Date:
Notes:

**310. Long-tailed
Skua**
*Stercorarius
longicaudus*
[Long-tailed Jaeger]
23 in 58 cms
V. May – No
I, S, SE, SW.

Place:
Date:
Notes:

311. Long-tailed Tit
*Aegithalos
caudatus*
5½ in 14 cms
R.
BI.

Place:
Date:
Notes:

**312. Long-toed
Stint**
Calidris subminuta
6½ in 16 cms
V. Jn – Au
I, N, SW. †

Place:
Date:
Notes:

**313. Macaronesian
Shearwater**
Puffinus baroli
[Barolo
Shearwater]
12 in 30 cms
V. Mar – De
BI. †

Place:
Date:
Notes:

**314. Macqueen's
Bustard**
*Chlamydotis
macqueenii*
26 in 65 cms
V. Oc – No
M, N, S, SE. †

Place:
Date:
Notes:

**315. Madeiran
Storm Petrel**
*Oceanodroma
castro*
8¼ in 21 cms
V. Oc
I. †

Place:
Date:
Notes:

**316. Magnificent
Frigatebird**
*Fregata
magnificens*
46 in 114 cms
V. No – De
M, N. †

Place:
Date:
Notes:

**317. Magnolia
Warbler**
*Setophaga
magnolia*
5 in 13 cms
V. Se
S, SW. †

Place:
Date:
Notes:

318. Magpie
Pica pica
[Eurasian Magpie]
18 in 45 cms
R.
BI.

Place:
Date:
Notes:

319. Mallard
Anas
platyrhynchos
23 in 57 cms
R.
Bl.

Place:
Date:
Notes:

**320. Mandarin
Duck**
Aix galericulata
17 in 42 cms
R.
M, N, SE, SW, W.

Place:
Date:
Notes:

**321. Manx
Shearwater**
Puffinus puffinus
14 in 36 cms
V. Fe - Oc
I, S, SW, W.

Place:
Date:
Notes:

**322. Marmora's
Warbler**
Sylvia sarda
5 in 13 cms
V. May – Jn
M, N, S, SE, W. †

Place:
Date:
Notes:

**323. Marsh
Harrier**
Circus
aeruginosus
[Western Marsh
Harrier]
21 in 53 cms
V. Ap – Oc
M, N, SE, SW.

Place:
Date:
Notes:

**324. Marsh
Sandpiper**
Tringa stagnatilis
10½ in 26 cms
V. Ap – Oc
BI. †

Place:
Date:
Notes:

325. Marsh Tit
Poecile palustris
4½ in 11 cms
R.
M, N, S, SE, SW, W.

Place:
Date:
Notes:

**326. Marsh
Warbler**
*Acrocephalus
palustris*
5 in 13 cms
V. May – Au
M, SE.

Place:
Date:
Notes:

**327. Masked
Shrike**
Lanius nubicus
7 in 18 cms
V. Se – No
N, S, SW. †

Place:
Date:
Notes:

**328. Meadow
Pipit**
Anthus pratensis
5¾ in 14.5 cms
R.
BI.

Place:
Date:
Notes:

329.
Mediterranean
Gull
Larus
melanocephalus
15 in 38 cms
R.
M, N, SE, SW.

Place:
Date:
Notes:

330. Melodious
Warbler
Hippolais
polyglotta
5 in 13 cms
V. Au – Oc
M, SW, SW.

Place:
Date:
Notes:

331. Merlin
Falco columbarius
13 in 33 cms
R.
BI.

Place:
Date:
Notes:

332. Mistle
Thrush
Turdus viscivorus
10½ in 26 cms
R.
BI.

Place:
Date:
Notes:

333. Moltoni's
Subalpine
Warbler
Sylvia subalpina
5 in 13 cms
V. May – Oc
S, SE, SW. †

Place:
Date:
Notes:

**334. Montagu's
Harrier**
Circus pygargus
17 in 42 cms
V. May – Aug
SE, SW.

Place:
Date:
Notes:

**335. Monteiro's
Storm Petrel**
*Oceanodroma
monteiroi*
7½ in 19 cms
V. Jl
SW. †

Place:
Date:
Notes:

336. Moorhen
*Gallinula
chloropus*
[Common
Moorhen]
13 in 33 cms
R.
BI.

Place:
Date:
Notes:

**337. Mourning
Dove**
Zenaida macroura
12 in 31 cms
V. Oc – No
I, S. †

Place:
Date:
Notes:

**338. Moussier's
Redstart**
*Phoenicurus
moussieri*
4¾ in 12 cms
V. Ap
W. †

Place:
Date:
Notes:

339. Mute Swan
Cygnus olor
60 in 150 cms
R.
Bl.

Place:
Date:
Notes:

340. Naumann's Thrush
Turdus naumanni
10 in 25 cms
V. Ja
SE. †

Place:
Date:
Notes:

341. Needle-tailed Swift
Hirundapus caudacutus
[White-throated Needletail]
8 in 20 cms
V. May – Jn
I, M, N, S, SE.

Place:
Date:
Notes:

342. Night Heron
Nycticorax nycticorax
[Black-crowned Night Heron]
24 in 59 cms
V. Mar – No
M, N, SE, SW.

Place:
Date:
Notes:

343. Nightingale
Luscinia
megarhynchos
[Common
Nightingale]
6½ in 16 cms
V. Ap – Se
M, SE, SW.

Place:
Date:
Notes:

344. Nightjar
Caprimulgus
europaeus
[European
Nightjar]
10½ in 26 cms
V. Ap - Se
M, N, S, SE, SW, W.

Place:
Date:
Notes:

**345. Northern
Harrier**
Circus cyaneus
hudsonius
18 in 45
V Oc - Mar
I, S, SE, SW. †

Place:
Date:
Notes:

**346. Northern
Mockingbird**
Mimus polyglottos
11 in 28 cm
V. May & Aug
SE, SW. †

Place:
Date:
Notes:

347. Northern Parula
Setophaga americana
4¾ in 12 cms
V. Se – No
I, N, S, SW. †

Place:
Date:
Notes:

348. Northern Waterthrush
Parkesia noveboracensis
6 in 15 cms
V. Apr & Au – Oc
I, M, SW. †

Place:
Date:
Notes:

349. Nutcracker
Nucifraga caryocatactes
[Spotted Nutcracker]
14 in 36 cms
V. Au – De
M, N, S, SE, SW, W. †

Place:
Date:
Notes:

350. Nuthatch
Sitta europaea
[Eurasian Nuthatch]
5½ in 14 cms
R.
M, N, S, SE, SW, W.

Place:
Date:
Notes:

351. Olive-backed Pipit
Anthus hodgsoni
6 in 15 cms
V. Oc - Ap
N, S, SE, SW, W.

Place:
Date:
Notes:

**352. Olive-tree
Warbler**
*Hippolais
olivetorum*
7 in 18 cms
V. Au
S. †

Place:
Date:
Notes:

**353. Oriental
Pratincole**
*Glareola
maldivarum*
9½ in 24 cms
V. May - Se
M, SE. †

Place:
Date:
Notes:

**354. Ortolan
Bunting**
Emberiza hortulana
6½ in 16 cms
V. Se – No
S, M, N, SE, SW.

Place:
Date:
Notes:

355. Osprey
Pandion haliaetus
[Western Osprey]
22 in 55 cms
V. Ap - Se
M, N, S, SE, SW.

Place:
Date:
Notes:

356. Ovenbird
*Seiurus
aurocapilla*
6½ in 16 cms
V. Se – De
I, M, S, SW. †

Place:
Date:
Notes:

357. Oystercatcher
Haematopus
ostralegus
[Eurasian
Oystercatcher]
17 in 43 cms
R.
Bl.

Place:
Date:
Notes:

358. Pacific Diver
Gavia pacifica
[Pacific Loon]
29 in 74 cms
V. No – May
I, M, N, S, SW, W. †

Place:
Date:
Notes:

**359. Pacific
Golden Plover**
Pluvialis fulva
10½ in 26 cms
V. May – No
Bl. †

Place:
Date:
Notes:

360. Pacific Swift
Apus pacificus
7 in 18 cms
V. May – Jl
M, N, SE. †

Place:
Date:
Notes:

**361. Paddyfield
Warbler**
*Acrocephalus
agricola*
5 in 13 cms
V. May – Oc
Bl. †

Place:
Date:
Notes:

**362. Pale-legged
Leaf Warbler**
*Phylloscopus
tenellipes*
4½ in 11 cms
V. Oc
SW. †

Place:
Date:
Notes:

**363. Pallas's
Grasshopper
Warbler**
*Locustella
certhiola*
5½ in 14 cms
V. Se – Oc
I, N, S, SE, SW. †

Place:
Date:
Notes:

**364. Pallas's Reed
Bunting**
Emberiza pallasi
5¼ in 13.5 cms
V. Jn – Oc
S, SE. †

Place:
Date:
Notes:

**365. Pallas's
Sandgrouse**
*Syrrhaptes
paradoxus*
16½ in 41 cms
V. Ja – De
Bl. †

Place:
Date:
Notes:

366. Pallas's Warbler
Phylloscopus proregulus
[Pallas's Leaf Warbler]
4¼ in 10 cms
V. Oc – Dec
M, N, SE, SW.

Place:
Date:
Notes:

367. Pallid Harrier
Circus macrourus
19½ in 48 cms
V. Mar – De
Bl. †

Place:
Date:
Notes:

368. Pallid Swift
Apus pallidus
6¾ in 17 cms
V. Mar – No
Bl. †

Place:
Date:
Notes:

369. Parrot Crossbill
Loxia pytyopsittacus
7 in 18 cms
V. No - Mar
N, M, SE.

Place:
Date:
Notes:

370. Pechora Pipit
Anthus gustavi
5¾ in 14.5 cms
V. Se – Oc
I, N, S, SW, W. †

Place:
Date:
Notes:

**371. Pectoral
Sandpiper**
*Calidris
melanotos*
9 in 23 cms
V. Au – No
BI.

Place:
Date:
Notes:

**372. Penduline
Tit**
Remiz pendulinus
[Eurasian
Penduline Tit]
4½ in 11 cms
V. Oc – Mar
SE, SW. †

Place:
Date:
Notes:

373. Peregrine
Falco peregrines
[Peregrine Falcon]
19 in 47 cms
R.
BI.

Place:
Date:
Notes:

374. Pheasant
*Phasianus
colchicus*
[Common
Pheasant]
33 in 83 cms
R.
BI.

Place:
Date:
Notes:

375. Philadelphia Vireo
Vireo philadelphicus
5 in 13 cms
V. Oc
I, SW. †

Place:
Date:
Notes:

376. Pied Flycatcher
Ficedula hypoleuca
[European Pied Flycatcher]
5 in 13 cms
V. Mar – Se
M, N, S, SW, W.

Place:
Date:
Notes:

377. Pied Wagtail
Motacilla alba
[White Wagtail]
7 in 18 cms
R.
BI.

Place:
Date:
Notes:

378. Pied Wheatear
Oenanthe pleschanka
5½ in 14 cms
V. Se – De
BI. †

Place:
Date:
Notes:

379. Pied-billed Grebe
Podilymbus podiceps
15 in 38 cms
V. Oc – Jn
BI. †

Place:
Date:
Notes:

380. Pine Bunting
Emberiza
leucocephalos
6¾ in 17 cms
V. Oc – Ap
Bl. †

Place:
Date:
Notes:

381. Pine
Grosbeak
Pinicola
enucleator
10 in 25 cms
V. Oc – May
M, N, S, SE. †

Place:
Date:
Notes:

382. Pink-footed
Goose
Anser
brachyrhynchus
30 in 75 cms
V. Oc – Ap
M, N, S, SE.

Place:
Date:
Notes:

383. Pintail
Anas acuta
[Northern Pintail]
22 in 55 cms
R. Ja – De
Bl.

Place:
Date:
Notes:

384. Pochard
Aythya farina
[Common
Pochard]
15 in 38 cms
R. Ja – De
Bl.

Place:
Date:
Notes:

385. Pomarine Skua
Stercorarius pomarinus
20 in 50 cms
V. Ap - No
BI.

Place:
Date:
Notes:

386. Ptarmigan
Lagopus muta
[Rock Ptarmigan]
14 in 35 cms
R.
S.

Place:
Date:
Notes:

387. Puffin
Fratercula arctica
[Atlantic Puffin]
12 in 30 cms
V. Mar – Au
I, N, S, SW, W.

Place:
Date:
Notes:

388. Purple Gallinule
Porphyrio martinicus
14½ in 37 cms
V. Ja/Ap/No
SE, SW. †

Place:
Date:
Notes:

389. Purple Heron
Ardea purpurea
36 in 90 cms
V. Mar – Jl
SE, SW.

Place:
Date:
Notes:

**390. Purple
Martin**
Progne subis
8 in 20 cms
V. Se
S. †

Place:
Date:
Notes:

**391. Purple
Sandpiper**
Calidris maritima
8¼ in 21 cms
V. De – Fe
I, M, N, S, SW, W.

Place:
Date:
Notes:

392. Quail
Coturnix coturnix
[Common Quail]
7 in 18 cms
V. Ap – Au
I, M, N, S, SE, SW.

Place:
Date:
Notes:

**393. Radde's
Warbler**
*Phylloscopus
schwarzi*
5 in 13 cms
V. Oc – No
S, SE, SW.

Place:
Date:
Notes:

394. Raven
Corvus corax
[Northern Raven]
25 in 62 cms
R.
I, N, S, SW, W.

Place:
Date:
Notes:

395. Razorbill
Alca torda
16 in 40 cms
V. Mar - Jl
I, N, S, SW, W.

Place:
Date:
Notes:

396. Red Grouse
Lagopus lagopus
[Willow Ptarmigan]
15 in 38 cms
R.
I, M, N, S, SW, W.

Place:
Date:
Notes:

397. Red Kite
Milvus milvus
24 in 60 cms
R.
I, S, M, N.

Place:
Date:
Notes:

398. Red-backed Shrike
Lanius collurio
6¾ in 17 cms
V. May – Oc
M, N, S, SE, SW.

Place:
Date:
Notes:

399. Red-billed Tropicbird
Phaethon aethereus
43 in 105 cms
V. May – Se
SW. †

Place:
Date:
Notes:

400. Red-breasted Flycatcher
Ficedula parva
4½ in 11 cms
V. May – No
Bl.

Place:
Date:
Notes:

401. Red-breasted Goose
Branta ruficollis
22 in 55 cms
V. Se – Ap
M, N, S, SE, SW, W.†

Place:
Date:
Notes:

402. Red-breasted Merganser
Mergus serrator
23 in 56 cms
R./V. De - Mar
Bl.

Place:
Date:
Notes:

403. Red-breasted Nuthatch
Sitta canadensis
4½ in 11 cms
V. Oc
SE. †

Place:
Date:
Notes:

404. Red-crested Pochard
Netta rufina
22 in 55 cms
R.
SE, SW.

Place:
Date:
Notes:

405. Red-eyed
Vireo
Vireo olivaceus
5½ in 14 cms
V. Se – No
I, N, S, SE, SW, W.†

Place:
Date:
Notes:

406. Red-flanked
Bluetail
Tarsiger cyanurus
5½ in 14 cms
V. Se – No
BI. †

Place:
Date:
Notes:

407. Red-footed
Falcon
Falco vespertinus
12 in 30 cms
V. Jl – Se
M, N, S, SE.

Place:
Date:
Notes:

408. Redhead
Aythya americana
14½ in 37 cms
V. Mar & Jl
I, M. †

Place:
Date:
Notes:

409. Red-legged
Partridge
Alectoris rufa
13½ in 34 cms
R.
BI.

Place:
Date:
Notes:

410. Red-necked Grebe
Podiceps grisegena
17 in 42 cms
V. De – Fe
M, N, S, SE, SW.

Place:
Date:
Notes:

411. Red-necked Nightjar
Caprimulgus ruficollis
12½ in 32 cms
V. Oc
N. †

Place:
Date:
Notes:

412. Red-necked Phalarope
Phalaropus lobatus
7 in 18 cms
V. May – Se
S, SE.

Place:
Date:
Notes:

413. Red-necked Stint
Calidris ruficollis
6¾ in 17 cms
V. Jl – Se
I, N, S, SE, SW. †

Place:
Date:
Notes:

414. Red-rumped Swallow
Cecropis daurica
6¾ in 17 cms
V. Ap – May
M, N, SE, SW.

Place:
Date:
Notes:

415. Redshank
Tringa totanus
[Common
Redshank]
11 in 28 cms
R.
BI.

Place:
Date:
Notes:

416. Redstart
*Phoenicurus
phoenicurus*
[Common Redstart]
5½ in 14 cms
V. Ap – Se
N, S, SE, SW, W.

Place:
Date:
Notes:

**417. Red-
throated Diver**
Gavia stellata
[Red-throated
Loon]
27 in 67 cms
V. Ap – Oc
I, S, W.

Place:
Date:
Notes:

**418. Red-
throated Pipit**
Anthus cervinus
5¾ in 14.5 cms
V. Au – De
BI.

Place:
Date:
Notes:

**419. Red-
throated Thrush**
Turdus ruficollis
10¾ in 27 cms
V. Se
SE. †

Place:
Date:
Notes:

420. Redwing
Turdus iliacus
8¼ in 21 cms
V. Se – Ap
BI.

Place:
Date:
Notes:

421. Reed Bunting
Emberiza schoeniclus
[Common Reed Bunting]
6 in 15 cms
R.
BI.

Place:
Date:
Notes:

422. Reed Warbler
Acrocephalus scirpaceus
[Eurasian Reed Warbler]
5 in 13 cms
V. Ap – Oc
I, M, N, SE, SW, W.

Place:
Date:
Notes:

423. Richard's Pipit
Anthus richardi
7½ in 19 cms
V. Se – No
M, N, S, SE, SW. †

Place:
Date:
Notes:

424. Ring Ouzel
Turdus torquatus
9½ in 24 cms
V. Mar – Se
BI.

Place:
Date:
Notes:

**425. Ring-billed
Gull**
*Larus
delawarensis*
19½ in 48 cms
V. De – Fe
I, SE, SW.

Place:
Date:
Notes:

**426. Ringed
Plover**
*Charadrius
hiaticula*
[Common Ringed
Plover]
7½ in 19 cms
R.
BI.

Place:
Date:
Notes:

**427. Ring-necked
Duck**
Aythya collaris
18 in 45 cms
V. De – Fe
BI.

Place:
Date:
Notes:

**428. Ring-necked
Parakeet**
Psittacula krameri
[Rose-ringed
Parakeet]
16 in 40 cms
R.
SE.

Place:
Date:
Notes:

429. River Warbler
Locustella
fluviatilis
5½ in 14 cms
V. Mar – Oc
M, N, S, SE, W. †

Place:
Date:
Notes:

430. Robin
Erithacus
rubecula
[European Robin]
5½ in 14 cms
R.
BI.

Place:
Date:
Notes:

431. Rock
Bunting
Emberiza cia
6½ in 16 cms
V. Fe – Oc
N, SE, W. †.

Place:
Date:
Notes:

432. Rock Dove /
Feral Pigeon
Columba livia
13 in 33 cms
R.
BI.

Place:
Date:
Notes:

433. Rock Pipit
Anthus petrosus
[Eurasian Rock
Pipit]
6¼ in 15 cms
R.
I, N, S, SW, W.

Place:
Date:
Notes:

**434. Rock
Sparrow**
Petronia petronia
6¾ in 17 cms
V. Jn
SE. †

Place:
Date:
Notes:

435. Rock Thrush
*Monticola
saxatilis*
[Common Rock
Thrush]
8 in 20 cms
V. Fe – No
I, N, S, SW, SE, W. †

Place:
Date:
Notes:

436. Roller
*Coracias
garrulous*
[European Roller]
12 in 30 cms
V. Ap – Oc
BI. †

Place:
Date:
Notes:

437. Rook
Corvus frugilegus
18 in 45 cms
R.
BI.

Place:
Date:
Notes:

**438. Roseate
Tern**
Sterna dougallii
15 in 38 cms
V. May – Au
I, N, S, SE, W.

Place:
Date:
Notes:

**439. Rose-
breasted
Grosbeak**
*Pheucticus
ludovicianus*
8½ in 22 cms
V. Se – De
I, N, S, SE, SW, W. †

Place:
Date:
Notes:

**440. Rose-
coloured Starling**
Pastor roseus
[Rosy Starling]
8½ in 22 cms
V. Oc – Mar
BI.

Place:
Date:
Notes:

441. Ross's Gull
*Rhodostethia
rosea*
12½ in 32 cms
V. Ap – Jn
I, N, S, SE, SW, W. †

Place:
Date:
Notes:

**442. Rough-
legged Buzzard**
Buteo lagopus
22 in 55 cms
V. May – No
M, N, S, SE.

Place:
Date:
Notes:

443. Royal Tern
Sterna maxima
20 in 50 cms
V. Jn – De
I, S, SW, W. †

Place:
Date:
Notes:

444. Ruddy Duck
Oxyura
jamaicensis
15½ in 39 cms
R.
BI.

Place:
Date:
Notes:

445. Ruddy
Shelduck
Tadorna
ferruginea
25 in 62 cms
V. Ja – De
SE, SW. †

Place:
Date:
Notes:

446. Ruff
Calidris pugnax
11 in 28 cms
R / V. De – Fe
BI.

Place:
Date:
Notes:

447. Rufous Bush
Chat
Cercotrichas
galactotes
[Rufous-tailed
Scrub Robin]
6 in 15 cms
V. Ap – Oc
I, M, N, SE, SW. †

Place:
Date:
Notes:

448. Rufous Turtle Dove
Streptopelia orientalis
[Oriental Turtle Dove]
14 in 35 cms
V. Oc - Mar
N, S, SE, SW. †

Place:
Date:
Notes:

449. Rufous-tailed Robin
Larvivora sibilans
5½ in 14 cms
V. Oc
S, SE. †

Place:
Date:
Notes:

450. Rüppell's Warbler
Sylvia rueppelli
5½ in 14 cms
V. Jn – Oc
S, SE, SW, W. †

Place:
Date:
Notes:

451. Rustic Bunting
Emberiza rustica
5¾ in 14.5 cms
V. Oc – Jn
I.

Place:
Date:
Notes:

452. Sabine's Gull
Xema sabini
13 in 33 cms
V. Jl – Fe
I, M, N, S, SE, SW.

Place:
Date:
Notes:

**453. Sakhalin
Leaf Warbler**
*Phylloscopus
borealoides*
4½ in 11.5 cms
V. Oc?
SW?.†

Place:
Date:
Notes:

454. Sand Martin
Riparia riparia
4¾ in 12 cms
V. Mar – Oc
BI.

Place:
Date:
Notes:

455. Sanderling
Calidris alba
8 in 20 cms
V. May – No
BI.

Place:
Date:
Notes:

**456. Sandhill
Crane**
Grus canadensis
49 in 122 cms
V. Ap & Se
I, N, S, SE. †

Place:
Date:
Notes:

**457. Sandwich
Tern**
*Sterna
sandvicensis*
16 in 40 cms
V. Mar – Se
BI.

Place:
Date:
Notes:

**458. Sardinian
Warbler**
*Sylvia
melanocephala*
5¼ in 13.5 cms
V. Mar – No
Bl. †

Place:
Date:
Notes:

**459. Savannah
Sparrow**
*Passerculus
sandwichensis*
6¾ in 17 cms
V. Ap, Se & Oc
S, SW. †

Place:
Date:
Notes:

460. Savi's Warbler
*Locustella
luscinioides*
5½ in 14 cms
V. Ap – Au
Bl. †

Place:
Date:
Notes:

**461. Scarlet
Rosefinch**
*Carpodacus
erythrinus*
6 in 15 cms
V. May – Se
M, N, S, SE, SW. †

Place:
Date:
Notes:

**462. Scarlet
Tanager**
Piranga olivacea
7½ in 19 cms
V. Se – Oc
I, S, SW. †

Place:
Date:
Notes:

463. Scaup
Aythya marila
[Greater Scaup]
19 in 47 cms
V. Oc – Mar
Bl.

Place:
Date:
Notes:

464. Scopoli's
Shearwater
Calonectris
diomedea
20 in 49 cms
V. Au
SW. †

Place:
Date:
Notes:

465. Scops Owl
Otus scops
[Eurasian Scops
Owl]
7½ in 19 cms
V. Mar – No
Bl. †

Place:
Date:
Notes:

466. Scottish
Crossbill
Loxia scotica
6¾ in 17 cms
R.
S.

Place:
Date:
Notes:

467. Sedge
Warbler
Acrocephalus
schoenobaenus
5 in 13 cms
V. Ap – Oc
Bl.

Place:
Date:
Notes:

**468. Semipalmated
Plover**
*Charadrius
semipalmatus*
8 in 20 cms
V. Ap & Se - Oc
I, S, SE, SW. †

Place:
Date:
Notes:

**469. Semipalmated
Sandpiper**
Calidris pusilla
6 in 15 cms
V. May – No
BI. †

Place:
Date:
Notes:

470. Serin
Serinus serinus
[European Serin]
4½ in 11 cms
V. Ja – De
SE, SW.

Place:
Date:
Notes:

471. Shag
*Phalacrocorax
aristotelis*
[European Shag]
30 in 75 cms
R.
I, N, S, SW, W.

Place:
Date:
Notes:

**472. Sharp-tailed
Sandpiper**
*Calidris
acuminata*
8½ in 22 cms
V. Jl – No
BI. †

Place:
Date:
Notes:

473. Shelduck
Tadorna tadorna
[Common
Shelduck]
26 in 64 cms
R.
BI.

Place:
Date:
Notes:

474. Shore Lark
Eremophila alpestris
[Horned Lark]
6½ in 16 cms
V. Oc – Ap
M, N, SE.

Place:
Date:
Notes:

**475. Short-billed
Dowitcher**
*Limnodromus
griseus*
12½ in 32 cms
V. Mar – No
I, N, S, SW. †

Place:
Date:
Notes:

**476. Short-eared
Owl**
Asio flammeus
16 in 40 cms
R. / V. De – Fe
BI.

Place:
Date:
Notes:

**477. Short-toed
Eagle**
Circaetus gallicus
[Short-toed Snake
Eagle]
27 in 67 cms
V. May – Oc
SE, SW. †

Place:
Date:
Notes:

478. Short-toed Lark
Calandrella brachydactyla
[Greater Short-Toed Lark]
5½ in 14 cms
V. Ap – Oc
M, N, S, SE, SW.

Place:
Date:
Notes:

479. Short-toed Treecreeper
Certhia brachydactyla
5 in 12.5 cms
R.
SE, SW. †

Place:
Date:
Notes:

480. Shoveler
Anas clypeata
[Northern Shoveler]
20 in 49 cms
R.
Bl.

Place:
Date:
Notes:

481. Siberian Blue Robin
Larvivora cyane
5½ in 14 cms
V. Oc
S, SE. †

Place:
Date:
Notes:

482. Siberian Rubythroat
Calliope calliope
6½ in 16 cms
V. Oc
N, S, SW. †

Place:
Date:
Notes:

483. Siberian Stonechat
Saxicola maurus
[Stejneger's Stonechat]
5 in 12.5 cms
V. Se – No
Bl. †

Place:
Date:
Notes:

484. Siberian Thrush
Geokichla sibirica
9 in 23 cms
V. Se – De
I, S, SE, SW. †

Place:
Date:
Notes:

485. Siskin
Spinus spinus
[Eurasian Siskin]
4¾ in 12 cms
R.
Bl.

Place:
Date:
Notes:

486. Skylark
Alauda arvensis
[Eurasian Skylark]
7 in 18 cms
R.
Bl.

Place:
Date:
Notes:

487. Slavonian Grebe
Podiceps auritus
[Horned Grebe]
13 in 33 cms
V. Jn – Fe
BI.

Place:
Date:
Notes:

488. Slender-billed Gull
Chroicocephalus genei
16 in 40 cms
V. Ap – Jl
SE. †

Place:
Date:
Notes:

489. Smew
Mergellus albellus
17 in 42 cms
V. De – Mar
SE, SW.

Place:
Date:
Notes:

490. Snipe
Gallinago gallinago
[Common Snipe]
11 in 28 cms
R.
BI.

Place:
Date:
Notes:

491. Snow Bunting
Plectrophenax nivalis
6½ in 16 cms
V. Se – Mar
I, M, N, S, SE, W.

Place:
Date:
Notes:

492. Snow Goose
Anser
caerulescens
28 in 70 cms
V. De – Fe
S, N.

Place:
Date:
Notes:

493. Snowy Egret
Egretta thula
24 in 61 cms
V. Oc
S. †

Place:
Date:
Notes:

494. Snowy Owl
Bubo scandiacus
24 in 61 cms
V. Ja – De
Bl. †

Place:
Date:
Notes:

495. Sociable Plover
Vanellus
gregarius
[Sociable Lapwing]
12 in 30 cms
V. Ja - De
Bl. †

Place:
Date:
Notes:

496. Solitary Sandpiper
Tringa solitaria
9 in 23 cms
V. Jl – Oc
I, M, N, S, SE, SW. †

Place:
Date:
Notes:

**497. Song
Sparrow**
*Melospiza
melodia*
7 in 18 cms
V. Ap - May & Oc
N, S, W. †

Place:
Date:
Notes:

498. Song Thrush
Turdus philomelos
9 in 23 cms
R.
BI.

Place:
Date:
Notes:

**499. Sooty
Shearwater**
Puffinus griseus
16 in 40 cms
V. Au – Oc
BI.

Place:
Date:
Notes:

500. Sooty Tern
*Onychoprion
fuscatus*
14 in 36 cms
V. Ap – Oc
BI. †

Place:
Date:
Notes:

501. Sora Rail
Porzana carolina
[Sora]
12 in 30 cms
V. Au – Ap
I, M, S, SE, SW, W. †

Place:
Date:
Notes:

502. Southern Grey Shrike
Lanius meridionalis
10 in 25 cms
V. Se – De
M, N, S, SE, SW. †

Place:
Date:
Notes:

503. Spanish Sparrow
Passer hispaniolensis
6½ in 16 cms
V. May – De
N, S, SE, SW, W. †

Place:
Date:
Notes:

504. Sparrowhawk
Accipiter nisus
[Eurasian Sparrowhawk]
15 in 38 cms
R.
Bl.

Place:
Date:
Notes:

505. Spectacled Warbler
Sylvia conspicillata
4¾ in 12 cms
V. Ap – Jn & Oc
N, SE, SW. †

Place:
Date:
Notes:

506. Spoonbill
Platalea leucorodia
[Eurasian Spoonbill]
34 in 85 cms
V. Ja – De
M, N, S, SE, SW.

Place:
Date:
Notes:

507. Spotted Crake
Porzana porzana
9 in 23 cms
V. Ap – Se
N, S, SE, SW.

Place:
Date:
Notes:

508. Spotted Eagle
Aquila clanga
[Greater Spotted Eagle]
29 in 74 cms
V. Oc – Ap
I, M, N, SE, SW. †

Place:
Date:
Notes:

509. Spotted Flycatcher
Muscicapa striata
5½ in 14 cms
V. Ap – Se
BI.

Place:
Date:
Notes:

510. Spotted Redshank
Tringa erythropus
12 in 30 cms
V. Jl – May
BI.

Place:
Date:
Notes:

511. Spotted Sandpiper
Actitis macularius
8 in 20 cms
V. Ap – De
BI. †

Place:
Date:
Notes:

512. Squacco Heron
Ardeola ralloides
18 in 45 cms
V. Ap – Oc
BI. †

Place:
Date:
Notes:

513. Starling
Sturnus vulgaris
[Common Starling]
8½ in 22 cms
R.
BI.

Place:
Date:
Notes:

514. Steller's Eider
Polysticta stelleri
18 in 45 cms
V. Aug – May
N, S, SE. †

Place:
Date:
Notes:

515. Stilt Sandpiper
Calidris himantopus
9 in 23 cms
V. Ap – No
BI. †

Place:
Date:
Notes:

516. Stock Dove
Columba oenas
13 in 33 cms
R.
BI.

Place:
Date:
Notes:

517. Stonechat
Saxicola rubicola
[European
Stonechat]
5 in 13 cms
R.
BI.

Place:
Date:
Notes:

518. Stone-curlew
*Burhinus
oedicnemus*
[Eurasian
Stone-curlew]
16 in 40 cms
V. Mar - Oc
SE, SW.

Place:
Date:
Notes:

519. Storm Petrel
*Hydrobates
pelagicus*
[European Storm
Petrel]
6 in 15 cms
V. May – Oc
I, S, W.

Place:
Date:
Notes:

**520. Subalpine
Warbler**
Sylvia cantillans
5 in 13 cms
V. Ap – No
I, N, S, SE, SW, W.

Place:
Date:
Notes: The Eastern
Subalpine Warbler
is illustrated.

521. Summer Tanager
Piranga rubra
6¾ in 17 cm
V. Se
W. †

Place:
Date:
Notes:

522. Surf Scoter
Melanitta perspicillata
20 in 50 cms
V. De – Fe
I, N, S, SW, W.

Place:
Date:
Notes:

523. Swainson's Thrush
Catharus ustulatus
8 in 20 cms
V. May & Se - Oc
I, S, SE, SW, W. †

Place:
Date:
Notes:

524. Swallow
Hirundo rustica
[Barn Swallow]
7½ in 19 cms
V. Mar – Oc
BI.

Place:
Date:
Notes:

525. Swift
Apus apus
[Common Swift]
6½ in 16 cms
V. Ap – Au
BI.

Place:
Date:
Notes:

**526. Swinhoe's
Petrel**
*Oceanodroma
monorhis*
[Swinhoe's Storm
Petrel]
8 in 20 cms
V. Jl – Au
I, N, S, SW. †

Place:
Date:
Notes:

**527. Sykes's
Warbler**
Iduna rama
5 in 13 cms
V. Jl – Oc
I, N, S, SE, SW. †

Place:
Date:
Notes:

**528. Taiga
Flycatcher**
Ficedula albicilla
4¾ in 12 cms
V. Ap & Se – Oc
N, S. †

Place:
Date:
Notes:

529. Tawny Owl
Strix aluco
15 in 38 cms
R.
M, N, S, SE, SW, W.

Place:
Date:
Notes:

530. Tawny Pipit
*Anthus
campestris*
6½ in 16 cms
V. Ap – No
I, SW.

Place:
Date:
Notes:

531. Teal
Anas crecca
[Eurasian Teal]
14 in 35 cms
R.
Bl.

Place:
Date:
Notes:

**532. Temminck's
Stint**
*Calidris
temminckii*
5¼ in 14 cms
V. May – Oc
M, N, SE, W.

Place:
Date:
Notes:

**533. Tengmalm's
Owl**
Aegolius funereus
[Boreal Owl]
10 in 25 cms
V. Oc – May
M, N, S, SE. †

Place:
Date:
Notes:

**534. Tennessee
Warbler**
*Oreothlypis
peregrina*
4½ in 11.5 cms
V. Se
S. †

Place:
Date:
Notes:

**535. Terek
Sandpiper**
Xenus cinereus
10 in 25 cms
V. Ap – No
Bl. †

Place:
Date:
Notes:

536. Thayer's Gull
Larus glaucoides
thayeri
26 in 64 cms
V. No – Mar
I, M, N, SE. †

Place:
Date:
Notes:

537. Thick-billed Warbler
Iduna aedon
6¾ in 17 cms
V. May & Se - Oc
S. †

Place:
Date:
Notes:

538. Thrush Nightingale
Luscinia luscinia
6½ in 16 cms
V. May – Oc
Bl. †

Place:
Date:
Notes:

539. Tree Pipit
Anthus trivialis
6 in 15 cms
V. Ap – Se
M, N, S, SE, SW, W.

Place:
Date:
Notes:

540. Tree Sparrow
Passer montanus
[Eurasian Tree Sparrow]
5½ in 14 cms
R.
I, M, N, S, SE.

Place
Date:
Notes:

**541. Tree
Swallow**
*Tachycineta
bicolor*
5¼ in 13.5 cms
V. May – Jn
S, SW. †

Place:
Date:
Notes:

542. Treecreeper
Certhia familiaris
[Eurasian
Treecreeper]
5 in 13 cms
R.
BI.

Place:
Date:
Notes:

**543. Trumpeter
Finch**
*Bucanetes
githagineus*
6 in 15 cms
V. May – Oc
N, S, SE, SW. †

Place:
Date:
Notes:

544. Tufted Duck
Aythya fuligula
17 in 42 cms
R.
BI.

Place:
Date:
Notes:

**545. Tufted
Puffin**
*Fratercula
cirrhata*
14 in 35 cms
V. Se
SE. †

Place:
Date:
Notes:

546. Turnstone
Arenaria interpres
[Ruddy Turnstone]
9 in 23 cms
V. Ja – De
BI.

Place:
Date:
Notes:

547. Turtle Dove
Streptopelia turtur
[European Turtle Dove]
11 in 28 cms
V. Ap – Se
M, N, SE, SW, W.

Place:
Date:
Notes:

548. Twite
Linaria flavirostris
5¼ in 13.5 cms
R / V. Ja – De
BI.

Place:
Date:
Notes:

549. Two-barred Crossbill
Loxia leucoptera
5¾ in 14.5 cms
V. Ja – De
BI. †

Place:
Date:
Notes:

550. Upland Sandpiper
Bartramia longicauda
12 in 30 cms
V. Ap – De
BI. †

Place:
Date:
Notes:

551. Varied Thrush
Ixoreus naevius
10½ in 26 cms
V. No
SW. †

Place:
Date:
Notes:

552. Veery
Catharus fuscescens
8 in 19.5 cms
V. May & Se - No
S, SW. †

Place:
Date:
Notes:

553. Velvet Scoter
Melanitta fusca
22 in 55 cms
V. Oc – Mar
Bl.

Place:
Date:
Notes:

554. Wallcreeper
Tichodroma muraria
6¾ in 17 cms
V. Mar – De
N, SE, SW. †

Place:
Date:
Notes:

555. Water Pipit
Anthus spinoletta
6¾ in 17 cms
V. Oc – Ap
M, SE, SW.

Place:
Date:
Notes:

556. Water Rail
Rallus aquaticus
11 in 28 cms
R.
BI.

Place:
Date:
Notes:

557. Waxwing
Bombycilla garrulous
[Bohemian Waxwing]
7½ in 19 cms
V. Oc – Mar
I, M, N, S, SE.

Place:
Date:
Notes:

558. Western Bonelli's Warbler
Phylloscopus bonelli
4½ in 11 cms
V. Ap – No
BI. †

Place:
Date:
Notes:

559. Western Orphean Warbler
Sylvia hortensis
6½ in 16 cms
V. May – No
N, SW, W. †

Place:
Date:
Notes:

560. Western Sandpiper
Calidris mauri
6¾ in 17 cms
V. Jl – No
I, S, SE, SW. †

Place:
Date:
Notes:

**561. Western
Subalpine
Warbler**
Sylvia inornata
5 in 13 cms
V. May – No
I, S, SW.

Place:
Date:
Notes:

562. Wheatear
*Oenanthe
oenanthe*
[Northern
Wheatear]
5¾ in 14.5 cms
V. Mar – Oc
Bl.

Place:
Date:
Notes:

563. Whimbrel
*Numenius
phaeopus*
16 in 40 cms
V. Ap – Au
Bl.

Place:
Date:
Notes:

564. Whinchat
Saxicola rubetra
5 in 13 cms
V. Ap – Se
Bl.

Place:
Date:
Notes:

**565. Whiskered
Tern**
Chlidonias hybrida
9¾ in 25 cms
V. Ap – Oc
Bl. †

Place:
Date:
Notes:

566. White Stork
Ciconia ciconia
40 in 100 cms
V. Ap – Se
SE.

Place:
Date:
Notes:

567. White's Thrush
Zoothera dauma
[Scaly Thrush]
11 in 28 cms
V. Se – Jn
I, M, N, S, SE, SW. †

Place:
Date:
Notes:

**568. White-bellied
Storm Petrel**
Fregetta grallaria
8½ in 22 cms
V. Se – No
SE, SW. †

Place:
Date:
Notes:

**569. White-billed
Diver**
Gavia adamsii
[Yellow-billed Loon]
39 in 97 cms
V. Oc – Ap
S.

Place:
Date:
Notes:

**570. White-
crowned Black
Wheatear**
*Oenanthe
leucopyga*
[White-crowned
Wheatear]
7 in 18 cm
V. Jn
SE. †

Place:
Date:
Notes:

571. White-crowned Sparrow
Zonotrichia leucophrys
7 in 18 cms
V. Ja, May, Oc
I, N, S, SE. †

Place:
Date:
Notes:

572. White-fronted Goose
Anser albifrons
[Greater White-Fronted Goose]
30 in 75 cms
V. Oc – Mar
I, M, S, SE, SW, W.

Place:
Date:
Notes:

573. White-rumped Sandpiper
Calidris fuscicollis
7 in 18 cms
V. Ap – No
I, M, N, S, SE.

Place:
Date:
Notes:

574. White-tailed Eagle
Haliaeetus albicilla
32 in 80 cms
R.
S.

Place:
Date:
Notes:

575. White-tailed Plover
Vanellus leucurus
[White-tailed Lapwing]
11½ in 29 cms
V. May – Jl
M, N, S, SE, SW. †

Place:
Date:
Notes:

576. Whitethroat
Sylvia communis
[Common Whitethroat]
6 in 15 cms
V. Ap – Oc
BI.

Place:
Date:
Notes:

577. White-throated Robin
Irania gutturalis
6½ in 16 cms
V. May – Jn
N, W. †

Place:
Date:
Notes:

578. White-throated Sparrow
Zonotrichia albicollis
7½ in 19 cms
V. Se – Jl
BI. †

Place:
Date:
Notes:

579. White-winged Black Tern
Chlidonias leucopterus
[White-winged Tern]
9¼ in 23.5 cm
V.Jn - Au
M, N, SE, SW.

Place:
Date:
Notes:

580. White-winged Lark
Alauda leucoptera
7½ in 19 cms
V. Oc – No
SE. †

Place:
Date:
Notes:

581. White-winged Scoter
Melanitta deglandi
24 in 60 cms
V. Fe/Ap, Jn &De
N, S. †

Place:
Date:
Notes:

582. Whooper Swan
Cygnus cygnus
60 in 150 cms
V. Oc – Mar
I, M, N, S, SE, W.

Place:
Date:
Notes:

583. Wigeon
Anas penelope
[Eurasian Wigeon]
18 in 45 cms
V. Ja – De
BI.

Place:
Date:
Notes:

584. Willow Tit
Poecile montana
4½ in 11 cms
R.
M, N, S, SE, SW, W.

Place:
Date:
Notes:

585. Willow Warbler
Phylloscopus trochilus
4¼ in 10 cms
V. Ap – Se
BI.

Place:
Date:
Notes:

586. Wilson's Petrel
Oceanites oceanicus
[Wilson's Storm Petrel]
7½ in 19 cms
V. Jl – Se
I, SW.

Place:
Date:
Notes:

587. Wilson's Phalarope
Phalaropus tricolor
9 in 23 cms
V. May – No
BI. †

Place:
Date:
Notes:

588. Wilson's Snipe
Gallinago delicata
11 in 28 cms
V. Se – Oc
I, SW. †

Place:
Date:
Notes:

**589. Wilson's
Warbler**
Cardellina pusilla
4¾ in 12 cms
V. Se – Oc
I, SW. †

Place:
Date:
Notes:

**590. Wood
Sandpiper**
Tringa glareola
8 in 20 cms
V. Ap – Se
I, M, N, S, SE, SW.

Place:
Date:
Notes:

**591. Wood
Thrush**
*Hylocichla
mustelina*
8¼ in 21 cms
V. Oc
SW. †

Place:
Date:
Notes:

**592. Wood
Warbler**
*Phylloscopus
sibilatrix*
5 in 13 cms
V. Ap – Au
BI.

Place:
Date:
Notes:

**593. Woodchat
Shrike**
Lanius senator
6¾ in 17 cms
V. Ap – Se
M, N, SE, SW.

Place:
Date:
Notes:

594. Woodcock
Scolopax rusticola
[Eurasian
Woodcock]
13½ in 34 cms
R.
BI.

Place:
Date:
Notes:

595. Woodlark
Lullula arborea
6 in 15 cms
R.
M, SE, SW.

Place:
Date:
Notes:

596. Woodpigeon
*Columba
palumbus*
[Common Wood
Pigeon]
16 in 40 cms
R.
BI.

Place:
Date:
Notes:

597. Wren
*Troglodytes
troglodytes*
[Eurasian Wren]
3¾ in 9.5 cms
R.
BI.

Place:
Date:
Notes:

598. Wryneck
Jynx torquilla
[Eurasian Wryneck]
6¾ in 17 cms
V. May & Au - Se
M, N, SE, SW.

Place:
Date:
Notes:

599. Yelkouan Shearwater
Puffinus yelkouan
15 in 38 cms
Jl
SW. †

Place:
Date:
Notes:

600. Yellow Wagtail
Motacilla flava
[Western and Eastern Yellow Wagtail]
6½ in 16 cms
V. Mar - Se
M, N, S, SE, SW.

Place:
Date:
Notes:

601. Yellow Warbler
Setophaga petechia
[American Yellow Warbler]
7 in 18 cms
V. Au – No
I, S, W. †

Place:
Date:
Notes:

602. Yellow-bellied Sapsucker
Sphyrapicus varius
8½ in 22 cms
V. Se – Oc
I, SW. †

Place:
Date:
Notes:

603. Yellow-billed Cuckoo
Coccyzus americanus
12 in 30 cms
V. Se – De
Bl. †

Place:
Date:
Notes:

604. Yellow-breasted Bunting
Emberiza aureola
6 in 15 cms
V. Au – Oc
Bl. †

Place:
Date:
Notes:

605. Yellow-browed Bunting
Emberiza chrysophrys
6 in 15 cms
V. May & Se - Oc
S, SE, SW. †

Place:
Date:
Notes:

606. Yellow-browed Warbler
Phylloscopus inornatus
4 in 10 cms
V. Se – No
Bl.

Place:
Date:
Notes:

607. Yellowhammer
Emberiza citrinella
6½ in 16 cms
R.
Bl.

Place:
Date:
Notes:

**608. Yellow-
legged Gull**
Larus michahellis
27 in 68 cms
V. Oc – Mar
SE, SW.

Place:
Date:
Notes:

**609. Yellow-
nosed Albatross**
*Thalassarche
chlororhynchos*
[Atlantic Yellow-
nosed Albatross]
32 in 80 cms
V. Jn
M, SW. †

Place:
Date:
Notes:

**610. Yellow-
rumped Warbler**
*Setophaga
coronata*
[Myrtle Warbler]
6 in 15 cms
V. Se – No
I, N, S, SW W. †

Place:
Date:
Notes:

**611. Yellow-
throated Vireo**
Vireo flavifrons
5½ in 14 cms
V. Se
SW. †

Place:
Date:
Notes:

INDEX

128